# ADAMIEL

## THE ENCOUNTER

ALEX TANGO

BALBOA.PRESS
A DIVISION OF HAY HOUSE

Balboa Press books may be ordered through booksellers or by contacting:

Balboa Press
A Division of Hay House
1663 Liberty Drive
Bloomington, IN 47403
www.balboapress.com
844-682-1282

Because of the dynamic nature of the Internet, any web addresses or links contained in this book may have changed since publication and may no longer be valid. The views expressed in this work are solely those of the author and do not necessarily reflect the views of the publisher, and the publisher hereby disclaims any responsibility for them.

The author of this book does not dispense medical advice or prescribe the use of any technique as a form of treatment for physical, emotional, or medical problems without the advice of a physician, either directly or indirectly. The intent of the author is only to offer information of a general nature to help you in your quest for emotional and spiritual well-being. In the event you use any of the information in this book for yourself, which is your constitutional right, the author and the publisher assume no responsibility for your actions.

Any people depicted in stock imagery provided by Getty Images are models, and such images are being used for illustrative purposes only.
Certain stock imagery © Getty Images.

ISBN: 979-8-7652-3976-6 (sc)
ISBN: 979-8-7652-3977-3 (e)

Library of Congress Control Number: 2023904076

Print information available on the last page.

Balboa Press rev. date:   02/28/2023

*This book is dedicated to*
*Mr. Makoto Anzai,*
*Allan Smythe,*
*and Mr. Shimisu.*

Silence is the kingdom of the soul, which is not seen by the human eyes.

November 14, 2012

Today I have been visited, and I have met Adamiel, a messenger.
I am for saying thus a king of my cosmos.
It is in another dimension very far from here.
We angels, we are pure beings, although not purer than God the Father.
Even so, we deserve respect
when we give our messages or when we are seen.

What level is your faith?
What level is your sincerity?
In what level is your delivery to others? To him?
Where stay you in this moment?
In the sand?
Does the water reach your ankles?
On the knees?
To the loin?
Or are you in the deep of the water?

Beloved one, I open my heart to you.

2.

Under the practice of longevity, you will meet immortality.

3.

Do not stress. Stress creates hunger.

4.

Basic tools: cleansing, purification, and transmutation.

5.

Meditation is a life of learning.
Meditation is alive.
Meditate daily. It will change your life.

6.

Every human is a child of the universe.

7.

Beloved one, make your heart your divine altar.

## 8.

Gaia wrote her laws in your heart.

9.

Talk with your angels. Call upon your divine angels. We are always in service to help.

## 10.

Free will is my own responsibility.

## 11.

Protect the sanctity of your own temple—your body.

12.

Angel of God, give me information.
Angel of God, give me inspiration.

## 13.
**Love is already in you.**

14.

Love yourself.
If you love yourself, your aura will emanate love.
Then you can talk about love.

15.

People look unconsciously for death, premature death,
because they don't know how to live.

16.

Everything we did in the past does not have reverse.
We have to wait and assume.

17.

Ways to control your mind: fasting, meditation, and relaxation.

# 18.

Fasting and meditation help to cleanse karma.

## 19.

Remember humans are a higher species.

## 20.

Your peace is awakened; your peace is wanted.

## 21.

The only one who is not interested in money is God.
Even so, that money is for everyone.

22.

The universe gives us the opportunities when we deserve them.
Keep going.

## 23.

Stay, and meditate.
Focus on the silence.
Seek the sound of silence.
Now go and focus. Go beyond.
And what will I find on the road?
Calm.

24.

God created man and woman, and he treats them the same.
We all deserve respect.
God only wants us to treat each other equal, regardless of our ignorance,
poverty, wealth, or intelligence and whether it is good or bad.
Everyone must be treated also.
We all deserve a good deal.

25.

Remember the people who help us. Take care of them, be more
attention to them, and be more grateful to them.

## 26.

God loves us and protects us.
Also, we must love and respect each other.
Transmit the love that God gives us.

27.

We are brothers despite our differences. God did not create racism.

## 28.

We always take a road in our lives.
Some are good, and some are bad.
Some people are not prepared, but at some time in their lives, the moment comes.

## 29.

In these moments, there are many ideas, projects, illusions, and thoughts.
The mind does not stop working at any time. Take everything calmly.
There is a lot of energy to achieve everything you want.

30.

God will see our effort; he will put opportunities in our
roads to be able to get where we want to go.

The paths in this life will be opening. There is no rush.

31.

To learn from ourselves, God always shows us a way.
It depends on us if we want to take it.

32.

The lies also block the evolution.
There are three great faults to the truth:
the lie
the deception
telling the truth and even exaggerating it

## 33.

On the road, someone seeks my help.
Support him. Do not open his eyes.
We are not wrong when we help someone.

34.

Message given by merlin the wizard.

You are doing things right.

Just keep calm.

Everything is coming little by little.

It is going to fall on you like rain, like the sky.

35.

When I remember, I just remember vanity. Now I am looking for just silence.

## 36.

You deserve to be the deity of such a temple.

## 37.

We can succeed without injuring or using those people, who we believe are below us.

## 38.

We only get there, and we only leave, some with the
satisfaction of having completed their mission.
It's time to start.
The time is now.

## 39.

Already feed the animal. Don't abandon it. You don't know
how great the protection it can give you can be.
Maybe within him is the person you never could be. Thank him, or
show him all the love you feel for him. It is time to forgive.

40.

You will enjoy a lot of peace and tranquility. Your heart chakra is more open to the sun.
Open your heart a little more. God could share all his love with all of us.
Why is it so hard to do it with our own family?

## 41.

Don't hurry. God has a time and a space for everything.

Avoid going forward. It may be harmful to your health.

**42.**

Share and give thanks. Be good to everyone.

43.

Archangel Raphael

Gather together, love, and respect each other.

It's time to give your hand to the one who has been in the mud for a long time.

By his bad words, go on there.

It's time to start.

It's time to create.

It's time to love us as brothers united, to build to destroy.

44.

It's OK. Life is like a labyrinth. We must stop and think which is the way to get out.
We must stop and choose well in order not to damage the people who surround us.

45.

God does not abandon his disciples.

### 46.

You must understand your project. It requires dedication and insulation,
not that you should leave your responsibilities to a side.

## 47.

### Message for a Tree

You feel our energy because you want to live like us. Do not waste your time. Live among us. Live like us, so that you fill yourself with love. Love yourself, and love others.

## 48.

Love is the deepest state of being.

49.

The judgment is the lack of prayer.

## 50.

We are their parents, not their masters.
They are our children, not our slaves.

51.

Fasting is sacrifice. God sees our sacrifices.
Overcoming an addiction is fasting.

52.

Spirit is love.
Spirit is healing.
Spirit comes from the divine.

53.

Here in my home, everything is peace.

54.

You can meet higher beings of light by meditation and by prayer.

## 55.

God does not care about the color of his sheep. He just wants no one to lose his flock.

56.

Enjoy the present.
It does not prevent you from being happy in the future.

## 57.

If you grow with love, you will gather the fruits that you never imagined.

## 58.

Have faith. Only in this way will the doors of the universe be opened; only thus will they make you the recipient of everything they have for you.

59.

There is no more than the present. Do not miss it by
criticizing, hating, judging, lying, and deceiving.
Enjoy it, love, laugh, forgive, and live now.

60.

Angel of God, fill my heart with light. Give me peace to forgive and to clean all the hate of those people who consciously or subconsciously have damaged me.

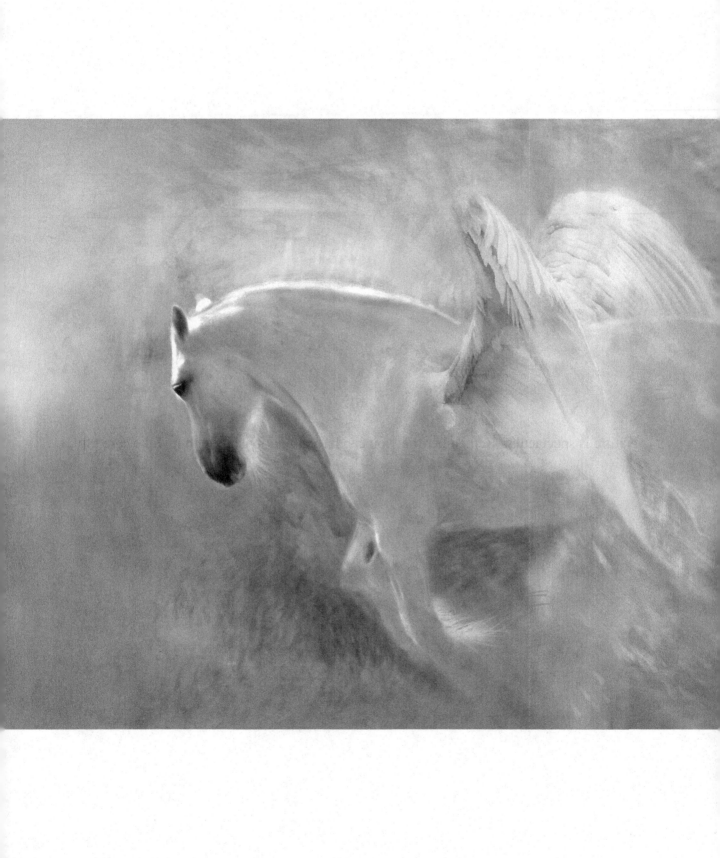

## 61.

Nature is spectacular. Remember that you can have a relationship with it. Take care of it.

62.

Share a smile at sunset, at sunrise.
Share life. This fills you with love.

63.

Help a person by listening to them without telling them what to do,
just listening without judging their mental interferences.

64.

Seeks to enhance your spiritual gifts every day.

65.

With will and discipline, you will conquer the mastery;
continue doing what you really like.

66.

A compassionate action cleanses family karma.

67.

Be patient, and have faith. Building something good takes time.

68.

With a good intention, you can enhance your gifts every day.

## 69.

Always bless the lord of the universe.

70.

Always vibrate. Resonate in the frequency of love.

## 71.

There are many kinds of miracles.
When you recognize the divinity within you, because you are
God, another miracle takes place in that moment.

72.

You create your own life.
You create your own future.
You create your own prophecy.

73.

We came to be teachers of all our being, to be teachers of ourselves, but sometimes we end up being masters of our drama and pain that we have created ourselves.

74

One of the true missions for which we are here is to remember.
Understand that God the Father is within us.

75.

God is not against money or abundance.
God always gives us abundance in different ways every day.

76.

Be still.
The Divine Spirit will answer.

## 77.

You are not alone. There are legions of angels chanting always your divine name.

## 78.

Divine Spirit, thanks for awakening me.

79.

A soul in fear feels lost, defeated. In that vibration, it is
away from the divine, from its own divinity.

## 80.

Blessed is the human being who takes his search
toward spiritual advance with discipline.

## 81.

What God wants is for us to have a pure heart.

## 82.

In a clean vessel, the divine will be channeled.

83.

Be your own hero.
Be your own miracle.
Be the pathway for your own miracles.

84.

Your spiritual evolution is my entire evolution too.
Your lies will slow your own process.
Your love will accelerate our own evolution.
Alone you are the microcosm.
Together we are the macrocosm.

85.

Abundance is the love of God in you.

## 86.

Be your own hero in your own day, in your own life, and in your own temple. So be it.

86.

When you are praying, the angels are with you.
Legions of angels.

87.

Be brave today. Embrace your spiritual gifts.

## 88.

God and your parents smile when they see your birth.

## 89

Today, take care of you.
Be reborn.

90.

Sleep is not for resting your body.
It's for regenerating your mind, body, and soul.

**91,**

When you are going to start something, your ego will start to talk and resist.
Get your mind and body ready to persist.

92.

You were born already for sure.
And you can be reborn. That is real too.
The new shifting starts from inside, from within.
You are the divine child.
You can vibrate in another rhythm.
You can change your breath by will.
Within, we are pure love.

We are beings of light.
We don't charge money; money doesn't exist for us.
I am always ready to help and to give advice.
Thanks.

Immortality is a gift from divinity.

We are here to guide.
We are here to help.
We are here to protect you.

When you are protected for a guide or for a spiritual being,
you don't have to pay for any message or guidance.
And you already have guides around you.

Only teach love.

Keep holy vibrations always in your heart.

Let all beings be peaceful.

Let all beings be blissful.

Let all beings be happy.

Be love.

Allow spirituality and divinity to be one with your physical state.

There is more light coming from the universe and from planet Earth to you.

Remember you are light.

Remember you are the divine child.

Pray always for knowledge and enlightenment.

Legion of angels of God the Father/Mother are bringing love to everyone.

You are always protected.

Printed in the United States
by Baker & Taylor Publisher Services